Searchlight BOOKS™

Fake News

What Are

Hoaxes and Lies?

Matt Doeden

Lerner Publications ◆ Minneapolis

Lerner Publications Company
An imprint of Lerner Publishing Group, Inc.
241 First Avenue North
Minneapolis, MN 55401 USA

For reading levels and more information, look up this title at www.lernerbooks.com.

Main body text set in Adrianna Regular.
Typeface provided by Chank.

Library of Congress Cataloging-in-Publication Data

The Cataloging-in-Publication Data for *What Are Hoaxes and Lies?* is on file at the
    Library of Congress.
ISBN 978-1-5415-5578-5 (lib. bdg.)
ISBN 978-1-5415-7473-1 (pbk.)
ISBN 978-1-5415-5668-3 (eb pdf)

Manufactured in the United States of America
1-46033-43356-4/11/2019

Contents

Chapter 1

HOAXES AND LIES ... 4

Chapter 2

A HISTORY OF HOAXES AND LIES ... 10

Chapter 3

HOAXES, LIES, AND SOCIAL MEDIA ... 18

Chapter 4

SPOTTING HOAXES AND LIES ... 24

Fake News Toolkit • 29
Glossary • 30
Learn More about Hoaxes and Lies • 31
Index • 32

PAGE PLUS Scan QR codes throughout for more content!

HOAXES AND LIES

In the 1930s, a picture captured the world's imagination. The search was on for the fabled Loch Ness Monster. People had reported seeing a huge beast in the waters of a lake in Scotland called Loch Ness. But nobody had yet snapped a photograph.

Robert Wilson said this photo showed the Loch Ness Monster.

Many people tried to capture the monster on film.

In April 1934, that changed. Robert Wilson snapped an image that showed something. Wilson claimed it was a photo of the monster. The image was splashed on newspapers around the globe. People argued about what it might be. Was it a dinosaur? A log? A trick of the light?

Only Wilson and a few others knew the truth. It was a hoax—a trick designed to fool people. The "monster" had been built out of a toy submarine. But that didn't stop it from being huge news, and the photo is still famous more than eighty years later.

The Basics

A hoax is an untrue story that is presented as true. A hoax is different from a mistake. To be a hoax, a story needs to be made just to fool people. The person who started the hoax spreads the false story on purpose.

President George H. W. Bush reads a hoax story about aliens in a newspaper.

Many hoaxes are harmless. A fake story about a Loch Ness Monster photo doesn't have a clear victim. People carry out harmless hoaxes for fun or just to see how others might react. Some are publicity stunts. In 2013, visitors to England's Charmouth Beach were stunned to find a giant dragon skull washed up onshore. News outlets ran with the fantastic story, but it proved to be a hoax. It was designed as a stunt to get attention for an online video streaming service.

Newspapers published stories about this giant skull that appeared at Charmouth Beach in 2013.

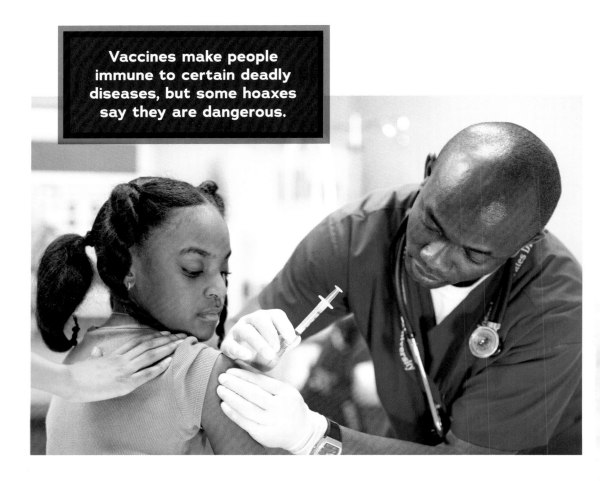

Vaccines make people immune to certain deadly diseases, but some hoaxes say they are dangerous.

Other hoaxes are harmful. What do false bomb threats do? They create terror, waste public safety resources, and interrupt daily life. Scam artists may invent hoaxes for financial gain. Hoaxes can cause people to act on false data.

In 1998, researcher Andrew Wakefield and his research team published a medical paper that linked vaccines to autism. Wakefield's paper was a hoax. He had made up the data. Yet his paper sparked a movement. Even after Wakefield's hoax was revealed, the anti-vaccination, or "anti-vaxxer," movement carried on. Supporters urged parents not to vaccinate their children. This opened the door for deadly diseases to spread.

Andrew Wakefield's medical paper proved to be a hoax.

Chapter 2

A HISTORY OF HOAXES AND LIES

Hoaxes and lies are as old as human history. But the invention of Johannes Gutenberg's printing press in the fifteenth century sparked a new era of hoaxes. The printing press made it easy to mass-produce news, including fake news. One of the earliest well-known hoaxes was the Drummer of Tedworth. The hoax spread in the mid-seventeenth century. It convinced many people that a drummer's ghost haunted a home in the English town of Tedworth.

A drawing from 1683 shows the Drummer of Tedworth (*in red above the house*).

This chess-playing machine hid a person who controlled the machine.

Another hoax caught the world's attention in the late eighteenth century. Wolfgang von Kempelen claimed to have built a machine that could play chess. The machine featured a mechanical man called the Turk. The Turk could beat most people in a game of chess. In truth, a real person who played chess hid under the table. This person controlled the machine. The Turk's skill was a wild claim, but for decades, people believed it was real.

Famous Hoaxes

In 1869, workers were digging a well in Cardiff, New York, when they found something amazing. It was a stone man that stood 10 feet (3.1 m) tall! People thought it was a giant that had turned to stone. This Cardiff Giant was big news. Scientists flocked to study it. But it was a fake. A New York man named George Hull had buried the fake remains as a hoax. He was making fun of people who believed giants once roamed Earth.

The Cardiff Giant was really just a stone carving of a large man.

In the 1930s in Wyoming, brothers Douglas and Ralph Herrick invented an animal. They mounted deer horns on the body of a jackrabbit. The jackalope was born! Locals knew it wasn't real. But tourists believed it. The myth of the jackalope spread. Many tourists came there to hunt the mighty jackalope!

The fake jackalope has become a symbol of Douglas, Wyoming.

Crop circles are detailed and beautiful hoaxes. These patterns of circles and lines began forming in fields in the 1970s. People wondered what they could be. Were they some strange natural event? Were they made by aliens trying to communicate? Books, TV shows, and movies explored the topic. The truth proved less interesting, however. Many were made by practical jokers.

One email hoax
involved tech
company Microsoft.

A chain letter said that Microsoft would pay email users for forwarding an email. Users would also be paid each time someone else forwarded the letter. Countless people were eager to cash in. They forwarded the letter to every contact in their inbox. The hoax grew and spread. Of course, it was nonsense. But the letter and the hopes of some easy cash live on in hoax emails and social media posts.

Social Media

In the twenty-first century, the rise of social media changed how people interact. Websites like Facebook and Twitter allowed people to connect in new ways. It didn't take long for such sites to become the center of the fake news world. Stories could spread like wildfire on social media. These stories did not have the fact-checking balance of mainstream media.

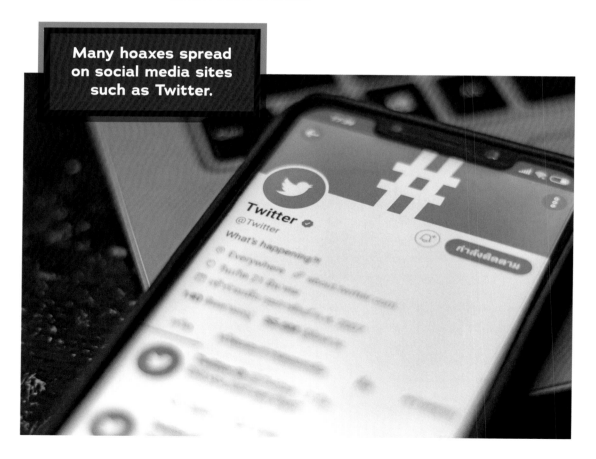

Many hoaxes spread on social media sites such as Twitter.

The idea of fake news grew with the rise of social media. A 2017 study showed that 62 percent of adults get at least some of their news from social media. These stories are shared from person to person. They may seem real, but often, they're not.

On social media, hoaxes can quickly go viral. In 2012, pranksters faked a photo of pop star Justin Bieber bald. They included a fake story that said Bieber had cancer and urged fans to shave their heads in support. Those who fell for it probably felt pretty silly when the story was revealed as a hoax.

A 2012 hoax involved pop star Justin Bieber.

Scams

Fake news on social media also has a dark side. Scam artists post fake stories to trick people into giving up personal information, passwords, or even money. They hack people's accounts and then ask their email contacts to send money to help with some emergency.

One of the most common scams comes with the promise of a big payday. A Nigerian prince wants to give a stranger millions of dollars, but he needs just a few hundred dollars to make the transaction. Those who fall for it send the money but never see their millions.

Some hoaxes involve large amounts of money.

Real or Fake?

Is this story real or fake? See the Fake News Toolkit on page 29 to help you decide.

Sasha Yang

July 19, 2015

I just saw a shark on the freeway in Rockville, South Carolina!

Like   Comment   Share

Fake! A poster put up a similar message, along with a fake photo of a shark swimming in hurricane floodwaters, in 2018. It's completely made up. A quick search would reveal that the same poster put up an identical message after a different hurricane in 2011.

Scan the QR code to try another example.

Chapter 4

SPOTTING HOAXES AND LIES

How can you tell when news is real and when it's fake? We live in an information age. News is everywhere. You can find it on TV, the radio, newspapers, and online. But not all news or news sources are created equally. Each of us needs to know how to spot fake news and what to do when we find it.

Legitimate news sites such as the BBC can be trusted, but not every story you read online is real.

A Skeptical Eye

When you're reading a news story, you've got to be a skeptic. This means that you expect proof before you believe a story rather than just accepting it as true. Being a skeptic doesn't mean you should disbelieve everything. It just means you should look at things with a critical eye.

How do you do it? Suppose you see a story online. Ask yourself about the source of the information. Is it from a reliable source? Does the story include complete information? Are any facts in the story backed up by sources that you can verify? If the answer to any of these questions is no, be skeptical.

Stick to the Facts

Hoaxes and lies come in all types. Some are easy to spot. Others seem very believable. To spot these, you'll need to check the facts.

Do a quick fact-check. Does something about a story seem questionable? Get online and search. Look on a reliable website, such as a major newspaper or museum. Do the research, consider the sources, and decide for yourself.

Be sure to fact-check what you read online.

You can find many reliable books at the library.

Be aware of your own bias as well. Everyone has ideas on issues. Don't let your biases affect how you see truth. Even if a story disagrees with a belief that you hold, judge it by the facts, not by your personal feelings.

You can't avoid hoaxes, lies, and fake news. They are a part of our culture. But a skeptic's eye can help you know what's real and what isn't.

Real or Fake?

Is this story real or fake? See the Fake News Toolkit on page 29 to help you decide.

See the Fake News Toolkit on page 29 to help you decide.

NEWS

Search

Tuesday, March 26

FRONT PAGE NEWS SPORTS VARIETY LIFESTYLE COMICS WANT ADS

DISAPPEARING BLACK HOLES

Black holes are one of the most fascinating objects in the universe. Their gravity is so strong that even light cannot escape them. Yet scientists have discovered that black holes don't last forever. According to late physicist Stephen Hawking, they evaporate over time! It takes billions of years, but even black holes don't last forever.

Real! It's true, according to Hawking and other top physicists. How could you know? The story gives a credible source, and an online search on Hawking and black holes would give you all the confirmation you need to know that this story is real.

Scan the QR code to try another example.

Fake News Toolkit

When you watch or read a news story, it can be difficult to spot fake news. People want you to believe what they believe. Many try hard to convince you, even if they have to lie or twist facts. Read on to arm yourself with some tools for spotting fake news.

Consider the Source

Does the news come from a respected media source? News items that come from little-known sources are more likely to be fake. Learn about the organization that published the story. Is its purpose to provide fair, objective news?

Look for Objectivity

If an article tells only one side of a story, it might be fake news. A good news story should look at an issue from all sides and let readers come to their own conclusions.

Check the Facts

Don't just accept any information that a news story gives you. Follow up. Find out where the information comes from. Do the figures and surprising facts presented come with sources? And if they do, can you follow up on them?

Don't Spread It

If you see a story that you think might be fake news, don't spread it! Don't like it or share it. Don't even click on it. The best way to make fake news go away is to ignore it.

Report It

Google, Facebook, and many other websites now have buttons that allow you to report fake news. If you are sure an item is fake, report it. That can help stop the spread of the story and prevent it from fooling others.

Glossary

bias: favoring some ideas or people over others

chain letter: a hoax, often in the form of an email or social media post, that tricks people into forwarding or reposting text with false claims

critical: the state of being aware of bias and flaws in something

mainstream media: traditional forms of communication and news, such as network television, newspapers, and radio

publicity: media coverage of a person, issue, or event

skeptic: a person who questions or doubts ideas or opinions

social media: websites that allow users to create and spread content

viral: a term that describes a story, video, or social media post that is very quickly and broadly shared

Learn More about Hoaxes and Lies

Books

Dakers, Diane. *Information Literacy and Fake News*. New York: Crabtree, 2018. What is fake news? How can you spot it? Learn more in this book.

Goldstein, Margaret J. *What Are Conspiracy Theories?* Minneapolis: Lerner Publications, 2020. Many people get caught up in conspiracy theories. How can we tell when a theory is fake news? Check out this book to find out more.

Young-Brown, Fiona. *Seeing through Internet Hoaxes*. New York: Cavendish Square, 2019. This title helps readers identify hoaxes online and provides resources for researching and debunking fake news.

Websites

FactCheck.org
https://www.factcheck.org
Is a story real or fake? Head to the website for articles and statistics that can help you decide.

How Newspapers Work
https://people.howstuffworks.com/newspaper.htm
How do newspapers find, collect, and distribute news? What kinds of checks and balances do they use to make sure news is real? Find out here.

How to Spot Fake News
https://kids.nationalgeographic.com/explore/ngk-sneak-peek/april-2017/fake-news
This website offers tips for spotting fake news and advice on how to deal with it.

Index

American Civil War, 15

anti-vaxxer movement, 9

Bieber, Justin, 21

chain letters, 18–19
crop circles, 14–15

Drummer of Tedworth, 10

Herrick, Douglas, 13
Herrick, Ralph, 13
Howard, Joseph, Jr., 15

jackalope, 13, 15

Kempelen, Wolfgang von, 11

Loch Ness Monster, 4–5, 7

Mallison, Francis, 15

Stringfellow, Douglas R., 16

Turk, 11

Wakefield, Andrew, 9
Wilson, Robert, 4

Photo Acknowledgments

Image credits: Bentley Archive/Popperfoto/Getty Images, p. 4; Trinity Mirror/Mirrorpix/Alamy Stock Photo, p. 5; PAUL J. RICHARDS/AFP/Getty Images, p. 6; PA Images/Alamy Stock Photo, p. 7; ER Productions Limited/Getty Images, p. 8; AP Photo/Charles Rex Arbogast, p. 9; Charles Walker Collection/Alamy Stock Photo, p. 10; Universal History Archive/Getty Images, p. 11; Pictorial Parade/Getty Images, p. 12; JonGorr/Getty Images, p. 13; Krzysztof Dac/Getty Images, p. 14; National Archives/Stocktrek Images/Getty Images, p. 15; Bettmann/Getty Images, p. 16; bgblue/Getty Images, p. 17; Grenar/Shutterstock.com, p. 18; Sundry Photography/Shutterstock.com, p. 19; Sattalat phukkum/Shutterstock.com, p. 20; Kevin Winter/DCNYRE2013/Getty Images, p. 21; IronHeart/Getty Images, p. 22; Alastair Pollock Photography/Getty Images, p. 23 (right); Diana Haronis dianasphotoart.com/Getty Images, p. 23 (left); Barrie Harwood/Alamy Stock Photo, p. 24; Goran Bogicevic/Shutterstock.com, p. 25; JGI/Jamie Grill/Getty Images, p. 26; Ariel Skelley/Getty Images, p. 27; vchal/Shutterstock.com, p. 28.

Cover: Heritage Images/Getty Images.